T0154510

The
SMALL and MIGHTY
Book of
Bugs

Published in 2022 by OH!.
An imprint of Welbeck Children's Limited, part of Welbeck Publishing Group
Based in London and Sydney.

www.welbeckpublishing.com

Design and layout © Welbeck Children's Limited 2022
Text copyright © Welbeck Children's Limited 2022

A CIP catalogue record for this book is available from the Library of Congress.

Writer: Catherine Brereton
Illustrator: Kirsti Davidson
Design and text by Raspberry Books Ltd
Product Manager: Russell Porter
Editorial Manager: Joff Brown
Design Manager: Matt Drew
Production: Melanie Robertson

ISBN 978 1 83935 192 1

Printed in Heshan, China

10 9 8 7 6 5 4 3 2 1

The
SMALL and MIGHTY
Book of
Bugs

Catherine Brereton and Kirsti Davidson

Contents

INTRODUCTION

~

This little book is absolutely bursting with facts about bugs.

Bugs are small animals that wriggle, crawl, creep, jump, fly, and scuttle and there are millions of different types.

The word "BUG" means a particular kind of insect with a mouth like a sharp straw, but lots of people use it to mean insects and other creepy-crawly minibeasts. That's how we'll use the word in this book.

Crawl inside these pages
and you will meet . . .

beetles that eat piles of poop

a spider that changes
colour to fool its prey

bees that dance

bugs that can walk on water

. . . and lots more.

You'll find that bugs come in all
shapes and sizes, from fleas
and tiny flies to huge tarantulas,
colossal beetles, and wide-winged
butterflies, and that they can do
some astonishing things.

Types
of
Bugs

Bugs include spiders, scorpions, millipedes, centipedes, woodlice, and insects. The scientific name for this group is **"ARTHROPODS"** —animals with no backbone, an armour-like skeleton on the outside of their body, and six or more jointed legs.

Insects are the biggest group of all. There are around a million different types of insects. There are **1.4 BILLION INSECTS** for every person on Earth.

The first insects appeared on Earth around **480 MILLION YEARS AGO.** That's around 170 million years before the first dinosaurs.

11

centipede

YOU CAN SORT BUGS ACCORDING TO HOW MANY LEGS THEY HAVE:

6 LEGS
insects

8 LEGS
spiders, scorpions,
and their relatives

14 LEGS
woodlice

30-750 LEGS
centipedes, millipedes

woodlouse

CATERPILLARS ARE YOUNG INSECTS, SO THEY HAVE **SIX LEGS.** THEY ALSO HAVE AN EXTRA EIGHT SOFT, LEG-LIKE THINGS CALLED "PROLEGS." THESE HELP THEM CLIMB AND CLING ON TO PLANTS.

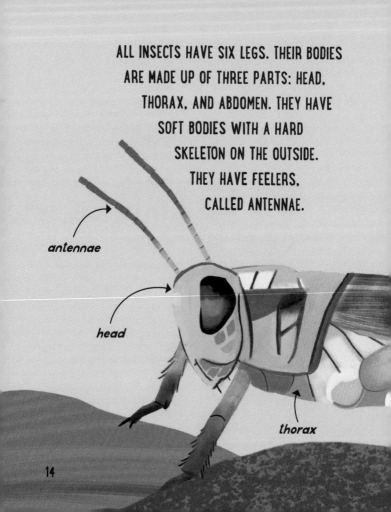

ALL INSECTS HAVE SIX LEGS. THEIR BODIES
ARE MADE UP OF THREE PARTS: HEAD,
THORAX, AND ABDOMEN. THEY HAVE
SOFT BODIES WITH A HARD
SKELETON ON THE OUTSIDE.
THEY HAVE FEELERS,
CALLED ANTENNAE.

antennae

head

thorax

14

MOST INSECTS HAVE WINGS, AND MANY
OF THEM ARE EXPERT FLIERS. SOME INSECTS HAVE
HARD WINGS WHICH THEY USE FOR PROTECTION,
AND OTHERS COMMUNICATE USING BRIGHT
COLORS ON THEIR WINGS.

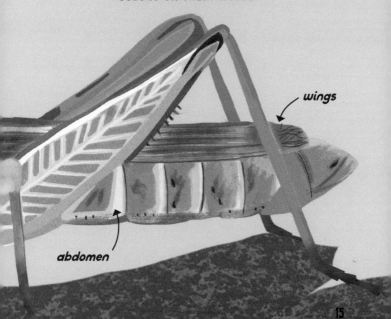

wings

abdomen

INSECTS

are divided into groups
—here are the six biggest:

BEETLES

BUTTERFLIES AND MOTHS

FLIES

ANTS, WASPS, AND BEES

TRUE BUGS

GRASSHOPPERS AND CRICKETS

There are around **300,000** to **400,000** different types of **beetle**. That's more than any other kind of animal on Earth. If you lined up all the different kinds of animal in the world, one in five of them would be a beetle!

Insects go through dramatic changes during their lives. For example, an adult butterfly and its young, a larva or caterpillar, are very different. They have different bodies and live different lives. Changing like this is called metamorphosis.

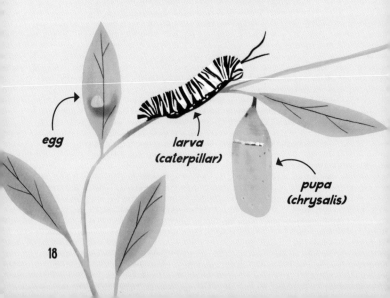

egg

larva
(caterpillar)

pupa
(chrysalis)

BUTTERFLIES HAVE A FOUR-STAGE LIFE CYCLE:

1. EGG

2. LARVA
(caterpillar)—an eating machine that eats and grows bigger

3. PUPA
(chrysalis)—a case inside which the caterpillar's body completely changes and turns into an adult

4. ADULT

adult

Some insects spend almost
their whole lives as

LARVAE

(which is the word for more than one larva).
Stag beetle larvae
eat and eat for around
seven years.

Adult mayflies
may live for only
ONE DAY.

DRAGONFLIES
have a three-stage
life cycle: egg,
nymph, adult.

SPIDERS' BODIES ARE MADE UP OF TWO PARTS:

A HEAD AND THORAX JOINED TOGETHER IN ONE, AND AN ABDOMEN.

Spiders produce silk.
They have little nozzles
on their abdomen called
SPINNERETS,
and this is where the silk
comes out from.

SPIDERS USE THEIR EIGHT LEGS FOR:

1. CAMOUFLAGE

2. HEARING, SMELLING, AND FEELING
(they have sound-, smell-, and movement-detecting bristles on the ends of their legs)

3. GRIPPING

4. TASTING

5. GROOMING (rather like a hairbrush)

6. CLIMBING

CENTIPEDES AND MILLIPEDES

are long, thin creatures with lots and lots of legs. "Centi" means "hundred" and "milli" means "thousand," but centipedes don't really have 100 legs and millipedes don't really have 1,000. Centipedes have between 10 and 300 and some millipedes have a whopping 750!

giant centipede

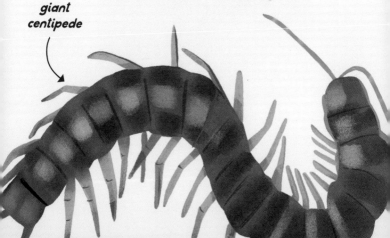

WOODLICE

are dry-land relatives
of shrimp and crabs. They
have 14 legs and hard armor
on their bodies. They need to live
where it is damp, so they
won't dry out.

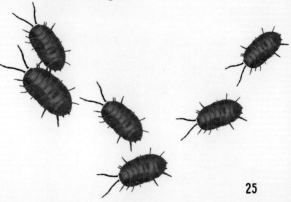

Feeding and hunting

BUGS

have some MARVELOUS MOUTHPARTS. Each type of mouth is exactly the right shape to do a precise job. Spiders have venomous fangs for injecting poison into their prey.

A house fly's mouthparts are like a tube with a sponge on the end. It VOMITS UP DIGESTIVE JUICES that turn its food to runny liquid, then uses the sponge to mop up the mess and slurp it up the tube.

house fly

shield bug

A **SHIELD BUG** has long, sharp mouthparts for piercing like a sharp straw or needle, leaves and **SUCKING OUT** the juice.

29

A GREAT DIVING BEETLE LARVA HAS HOLLOW JAWS. IT USES THEM TO SQUIRT DIGESTIVE JUICES INTO ITS PREY'S BODY. THE JUICES TURN THE PREY INTO SOUPY MUSH AND THEN THE BEETLE LARVA SUCKS UP THE MUSH. THIS MEANS IT CAN EAT ANIMALS QUITE A LOT BIGGER THAN ITSELF.

A bee has multipurpose mouthparts. It has jaws for **CHEWING, DIGGING, AND SHAPING WAX.** It has a long tongue which joins up with the jaws to make a tube for sucking up nectar.

Mosquito larvae have feathery, bristle-like mouthparts for filtering **TINY SCRAPS** of food out of water.

great diving beetle (adult)

The insect with the
longest tongue is

WALLACE'S SPHINX MOTH

found in Madagascar. Its
tongue is 11 in. long, which
is more than four times as
long as its body. Like other
butterflies and moths, most
of the time it keeps its
tongue curled up.

THE SCIENTIST
CHARLES DARWIN
AND OTHERS PREDICTED THIS
MOTH WOULD EXIST BEFORE
THEY EVER SAW ONE BECAUSE
THERE'S A FLOWER WITH A
12 IN. LONG NECTAR TUBE.
THE SCIENTISTS THOUGHT
THERE MUST BE A MOTH WITH
A TONGUE LONG ENOUGH TO
REACH INSIDE THE FLOWER.

CATERPILLARS

are eating machines! Their bodies are just a long tube for moving to find food and for eating **and eating . . . and eating.** From the moment they hatch, they eat, grow, and shed their skin so they have room to eat and grow **even more.**

Ladybug larvae look like little aliens, and if you were a greenfly you might think they were out-of-this-world scary!

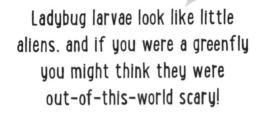

Each larva can eat up to 250 greenfly every day!

Some adult insects **don't eat at all.**
An adult **LUNA MOTH** doesn't even
have a mouth. It lives off the
food it ate while it was a caterpillar.

stag beetle

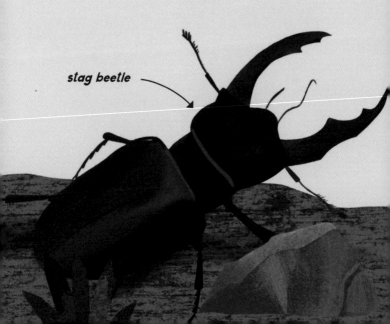

We don't know whether adult **STAG BEETLES** eat anything. They use their **impressive mouthparts for fighting.** Males wrestle with each other using their long jaws like stags' antlers.

There are around 7,000 different beetles that only eat DUNG. This may sound gross, but it's a very important job.

Imagine how much animal poop would be piled up all over the Earth if dung beetles weren't there to deal with it!

FIVE BUGS THAT EAT BLOOD:

1. Bedbugs
2. Fleas
3. Headlice
4. Mosquitoes
5. Ticks

THE VAMPIRE SPIDER FEEDS ON MOSQUITOES THAT HAVE SUCKED BLOOD.

DRAGONFLIES ARE AMAZING HUNTERS. THEY HAVE:

- ENORMOUS EYES WITH UP TO 30,000 INDIVIDUAL LENSES

- THE ABILITY TO SEE IN A COMPLETE CIRCLE AROUND THEM

- WINGS THAT ALLOW THEM TO FLY FORWARD, BACKWARD, UPSIDE DOWN, HOVER IN ONE PLACE, OR TURN SHARP CORNERS

- SPEED—THEY ARE SOME OF THE FASTEST FLIERS IN THE INSECT WORLD

- JAWS THAT CAN OPEN AS WIDE AS THEIR WHOLE HEAD.

~

The
TIGER BEETLE
is one of the fastest
hunters in the insect world.
It races across sand dunes to
catch spiders, tiger caterpillars
and ants, at speeds of more than
5 MPH, which means
it is hurtling along at
125 times its own body
length every second.

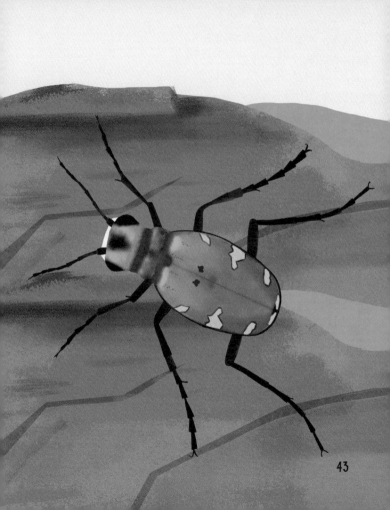

43

PRAYING MANTISES ARE VERY SUCCESSFUL PREDATORS. THESE ARE THEIR WEAPONS:

1. Many kinds are brilliantly camouflaged so they can lie in wait for their prey.

2. They can turn their head all the way around to see what's coming.

3. They move their legs with lightning speed to catch prey when it appears, and hold it very tightly with saw-like front legs.

Some mantises can eat prey much bigger than themselves.

An orb web is the **BIG**, round type of web that looks like a bicycle wheel. The "spokes" are strong threads that make the framework of the web and the rings are made of sticky threads for catching prey.

The spider sits in the middle of the web and when something lands, the spider feels the strands shake. Then it uses venomous fangs to paralyze the trapped prey before eating it.

Orb webs are not the only web shapes. There are sheet webs, tangle webs, funnel webs, and a few others.

jumping
spider

JUMPING SPIDERS

DON'T USE WEBS AT ALL. THEY JUMP, LEAPING UP TO 50 TIMES THEIR BODY LENGTH TO POUNCE ON THEIR PREY. THEY SPIN A LINE OF SILK WHICH ACTS A BIT LIKE A SAFETY NET, HELPING THEM TO LAND SMOOTHLY.

Instead of a web, a trapdoor spider builds a burrow that has a **TRAPDOOR WITH A SPRING SPUN OUT OF SILK.** It leaves the door half-open, waiting for an insect to go by. Then it rushes out, pulls the insect into its burrow, and slams the trapdoor shut.

Camouflage
and
Communication

Many bugs are **MASTERS OF DISGUISE**. Some are camouflaged to match their surroundings, so they blend in with the background and can hide from predators or prey. This is called cryptic coloring.

THREE BUGS THAT BLEND IN WITH GREENERY:

1. Grasshopper— blends into grass

2. Greenfly—blends in against buds, young leaves, and stems

3. Green shield bug—blends in with young green leaves in summer, brown leaves in autumn

52

The flower crab spider can change color to match the flower it hides in.

MANY BUGS DISGUISE THEMSELVES
AS OTHER OBJECTS—SUCH AS A
LEAF OR TWIG—OR LIKE OTHER,
MORE DANGEROUS ANIMALS.
THIS IS CALLED MIMICRY.

THIS STICK INSECT LOOKS JUST
LIKE A STICK. ITS A WOODY
BROWN COLOR WITH A LONG, THIN
BODY AND LEGS. IT EVEN SWAYS
LIKE A STICK SWAYING
IN THE BREEZE.

THE SNAKE MIMIC HAWKMOTH
CATERPILLAR LOOKS LIKE A SNAKE.

SOME BUGS MAKE A
KIND OF FANCY DRESS AS
THEIR CAMOUFLAGE. THE
GREEN TORTOISE BEETLE
LARVA ARRANGES DEAD
SKIN AND DROPPINGS ON
SPIKES ON ITS BACK.

WHEN LACEWING LARVAE
HAVE SUCKED OUT THE
INSIDES OF THEIR PREY,
GREENFLY, THEY PILE UP
THE DRIED-UP BODIES
ON THEIR BACKS FOR
CAMOUFLAGE. THEY ARE
HIDING FROM ANTS THAT
USUALLY PROTECT
THE GREENFLY.

Many bugs use warning colors, which shout out the message,

"DANGER—
KEEP AWAY!"

They may be poisonous or yucky to eat, or they may have a nasty bite or sting.

STRIPY MONARCH CATERPILLARS eat a plant that contains a chemical that in turn makes them poisonous to eat. The adult butterflies are poisonous too, and have black and orange warning colors.

Common warning colors are **BLACK AND WHITE, RED, YELLOW, AND ORANGE.**

59

SOME BUGS that use warning colors are not telling the TRUTH!

They are not dangerous, but have warning colors so they look like another bug that does. This fools predators into leaving them alone. Hoverflies (which look like wasps or bees) and many butterflies are good examples.

60

IT'S NOT ONLY BUGS THAT USE WARNING
COLORS. ELSEWHERE IN THE ANIMAL KINGDOM,
MANY RAINFOREST FROGS HAVE BRIGHTLY
COLORED, POISONOUS SKIN. THERE ARE
NON-POISONOUS FROGS WITH ALMOST THE SAME
COLOR PATTERNS. THE CORAL SNAKE
IS EXTREMELY VENOMOUS. THE MILK SNAKE,
WHICH LOOKS VERY SIMILAR, IS NOT.

TIGER STRIPES

are a very common warning
pattern. In South America there
are 200 different kinds of butterfly
that have black and orange stripes.
Some of them are poisonous,
but birds learn to avoid
all of them.

FIVE STRIPY BUGS THAT AREN'T WASPS OR BEES:

1. HOVERFLY
2. ZEBRA SPIDER
3. RAINBOW LEAF BEETLE
4. GOLDEN-RINGED DRAGONFLY
5. TEN-LINED JUNE BEETLE

rainbow leaf beetle

black and
yellow
longhorn
beetle

FIVE SPOTTED BUGS:

1. Ladybug
2. Domino beetle
3. Black and yellow
   longhorn beetle
4. Speckled wood
   butterfly
5. Burnet moth

LADYBUGS can pretend to be **DEAD**
so that predators will avoid them. They lie
on their backs with their legs up in the air,
and even produce small blobs of
bad-smelling yellow blood.

ANIMAL COLORS ARE NOT JUST FOR HIDING FROM
PREDATORS OR PREY. THEY ARE SOMETIMES USED
FOR SHOWING OFF AND FINDING A MATE.

Bright colors help
butterflies stand out
AGAINST THEIR SURROUNDINGS.
Other butterflies can recognize
them and know who is a
male and who is
a female.

THE SAME IS TRUE OF

DRAGONFLIES,

WHERE THE PATTERNS ON MALES' WINGS
IMPRESS AND ATTRACT FEMALES.

FEMALE BUTTERFLIES
CHOOSE THEIR MATES PARTLY BY SMELL.
THE MALES PRODUCE A PERFUME
THAT THE FEMALES LOVE, AND THEY
USE **SPECIAL SCALES**
ON THEIR WINGS TO WAFT
THE PERFUME INTO THE AIR.

antennae
for smelling

Female moths wear perfume to
attract mates, too. A male emperor
moth can smell a female more than
6.5 mi. away and can follow
the scent to find her.

Many insects find their
food using smell.

DUNG BEETLES

can smell fresh cow pats
just minutes after they
have plopped onto
the ground.

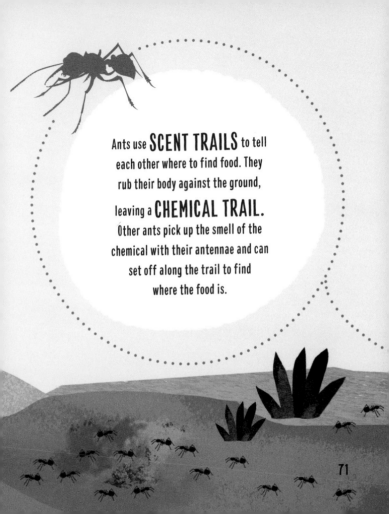

Ants use **SCENT TRAILS** to tell each other where to find food. They rub their body against the ground, leaving a **CHEMICAL TRAIL.** Other ants pick up the smell of the chemical with their antennae and can set off along the trail to find where the food is.

71

A QUEEN WASP USES SMELL TO KEEP OTHER WASPS IN HER NEST UNDER CONTROL. SHE GIVES OFF A SMELLY CHEMICAL THAT SOOTHES THE OTHER WASPS AND TELLS THEM TO DO THEIR JOBS. THE WORKERS DO THEIR JOBS AND DON'T ATTACK THE QUEEN. BUT WHEN THE QUEEN GETS OLD AND PRODUCES LESS OF THE CHEMICAL, THE OTHER WASPS GET RESTLESS.

QUEEN ANTS, QUEEN BEES,
AND QUEEN TERMITES USE
SMELL TO KEEP
THEIR WORKERS UNDER
CONTROL, TOO!

MALE **GRASSHOPPERS** and **CRICKETS** chirp and sing to attract females. They're also saying to other males, "Keep away —this is my territory."

grasshopper

74

GRASSHOPPERS sing by using their body like a violin. They use their back legs, which have a row of tiny pegs on them, like the violin bow, rubbing them against their front wings to make a sound.

75

CRICKETS CHIRP

BY RUBBING THEIR WINGS
TOGETHER. ONE WING HAS
A JAGGED EDGE CALLED
A SCRAPER, WHICH THEY
RUB AGAINST THE RIB OF
ANOTHER WING. IT'S A
BIT LIKE RUNNING YOUR
FINGER ALONG THE
TEETH OF A COMB.

MOLE CRICKETS

hide underground, but they still
need their chirps to be heard.
They build a specially shaped
chamber that works like a
LOUDSPEAKER and helps

Glow worms (which are not worms, but beetles) communicate using sparkly light displays. Only the females glow. The tip of their abdomen glows green in the dark, acting as a signal to draw males toward them.

FIREFLIES are also glow-in-the-dark beetles.
They gather in great swarms, creating an amazing flickering display when thousands of male fireflies flash their lights at once. The message is, "I'm here and ready to find a mate."

glow worm

HONEYBEES

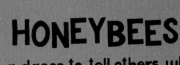

do a dance to tell others where they have found food. When a honeybee comes back to the hive, she waggles her body in a figure-of-eight pattern.

The other honeybees can tell how far away the food is by **HOW LONG HER DANCE LASTS.** They know exactly where it is from the angle at which she holds her body as she dances.

81

SCORPIONS

dance when they are getting ready to mate. The male and female hold each other's claws and dance. It's a way for the female to find out if the male is strong enough for her liking.

MALE PEACOCK SPIDERS

dance to attract females.
These tiny Australian spiders
have bright, rainbow-colored
flaps on their bodies.

They lift these up like a peacock's
tail fan and show off their best
moves. If the female is not
impressed, she might attack
and eat him!

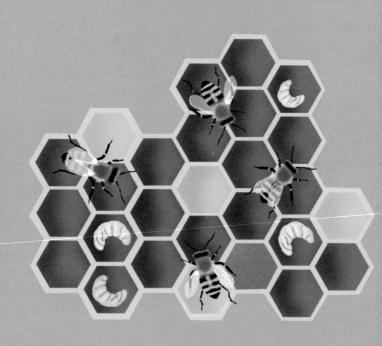

Bug Homes, Nests, and Eggs

ANTS, TERMITES, and SOME BEES
and WASPS live in groups called colonies,
made up of thousands or even millions
of individuals. They build impressive
homes with clever, complicated design
features. In the colony, the different
members have different
jobs to do.

IN A COLONY, THERE ARE:

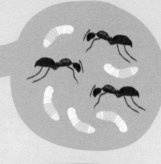

WORKERS—FEMALES WHO
LOOK AFTER THE NEST AND
YOUNG, FORAGE FOR FOOD,
AND PROTECT THE COLONY

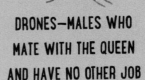

DRONES—MALES WHO
MATE WITH THE QUEEN
AND HAVE NO OTHER JOB

QUEEN—A FEMALE
WHO LAYS EGGS

87

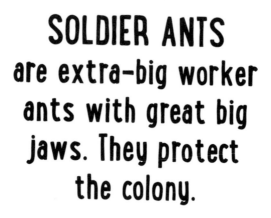

SOLDIER ANTS
are extra-big worker
ants with great big
jaws. They protect
the colony.

There are about
100 TRILLION
ants on the planet.

Usually, worker ants build the nest. But with

WEAVER ANTS

even the grubs join in. These ants build their nests by joining together leaves that are still growing on trees. Hundreds of workers pull together to drag and hold the leaves in place.

The weaver ants take hold of
LARVAE,
squeeze them a bit so that
they produce gluey silk, and
stick the leaves together
to make the nest.

worker bee

BUSY HONEYBEE WORKERS
DO A LOT OF DIFFERENT JOBS
AT DIFFERENT TIMES IN THEIR
LIVES. THESE ARE THE FOUR
MAIN PHASES:

1. Cleaning the cell they were born in, ready for another egg

2. Feeding the larvae, around 10,000 times a day, and tending to the queen

3. Making honey from nectar other bees bring into the hive, making wax for building, storing food, guarding the hive entrance

4. Foraging—flying out to find nectar and pollen

A **QUEEN TERMITE**
CAN LAY MORE THAN
**30,000 EGGS
A DAY.** SHE LIVES FOR 15
YEARS, SO CAN LAY PERHAPS
165 MILLION EGGS
IN HER LIFE!

94

SHE IS SO BIG THAT
SHE CAN'T MOVE AT ALL,
AND RELIES ON MILLIONS
OF WORKERS TO FEED
HER, GROOM HER,
CARRY HER EGGS AND
WASTE AWAY, AND
EVEN LICK HER
SWEAT (YUCK!).

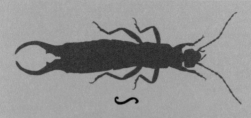

MOTHER EARWIGS

tend their eggs. They keep them warm through the winter, protect them from predators, and keep them clean. When they hatch, moms feed the young until they can feed themselves.

FATHER GIANT
WATER BUGS

TAKE CARE OF THEIR EGGS. THE FEMALE
LAYS EGGS ON HIS BACK. HE DOES
UNDERWATER PUSH-UPS AND SWIMS
UP AND DOWN TO THE SURFACE WITH
THE EGGS. THIS IS TO MAKE SURE
THEY HAVE FRESH FLOWING WATER
AROUND THEM AT ALL TIMES.

MOST BUGS DONT LOOK AFTER
THEIR EGGS OR BABIES AT ALL.

Spiders spin

SILK NESTS

for their eggs.

A mother

NURSERY
WEB SPIDER

carries her nest around with her.
She spins a silk egg sac and carries it
around in her jaws. This means she
can't eat anything until her
eggs have hatched.

A BABY SPIDER
IS CALLED A
SPIDERLING.

Special
Bug
Skills

BUTTERFLIES, BEES,
AND HOVERFLIES CAN SEE
ULTRAVIOLET LIGHT, SO
THEY CAN SEE PATTERNS ON FLOWERS
THAT WE CAN'T SEE. THE PATTERNS
POINT THEM TOWARD THE SUGARY
NECTAR INSIDE
THE FLOWERS.

WE CAN ONLY SEE
COMBINATIONS OF RED, GREEN,
AND BLUE BUT DRAGONFLIES CAN
SEE 11 DIFFERENT COLORS INCLUDING
ULTRAVIOLET. THEIR BIG EYES
GIVE THEM NEARLY AN
ALL-ROUND VIEW.

Sweat bees live in the rainforests of South America. They fly at night and can see in the dark. Their eyes are 27 times more sensitive to light than other bees' are.

People designing

DRONES

try to work out how to
make them fly fast, fly up,
down, forward, backward,
stop in mid-air, and change
direction swiftly. They
study dragonflies, which
can do all these things.

drone

dragonfly

Tiny **MONEY SPIDERS** can "fly" up to 10,000 ft. in the air—that's higher than some mountains and clouds. They spin a line of silk which is whipped up by the wind, then they drift through the air like a kite.

MONARCH BUTTERFLIES ARE **CHAMPIONS OF MIGRATION.** EACH YEAR HUGE SWARMS OF THEM TRAVEL **THOUSANDS OF MILES,** SOME JOURNEYING 2,800 MI. FROM MEXICO TO CANADA. BUT NO INDIVIDUAL BUTTERFLY COMPLETES THE WHOLE TRIP THERE AND BACK. IT'S **LIKE A FAMILY RELAY.** A BUTTERFLY THAT RETURNS "HOME" FOR WINTER WILL BE THE GREAT-GRANDCHILD OF ONE THAT SET OFF IN SPRING.

A **MONARCH** CAN FLY ABOUT **25-30 MI.** EVERY DAY.

They find their way using a built-in **"COMPASS"** in their **ANTENNAE.**

Many insects are experts at navigation.

Ants use patterns and landmarks to remember the routes to different sources of food. One type of African savanna dung beetle uses the pattern of the Milky Way in the night sky to help it find its way.

SPIDERS' SUPERPOWER IS MAKING SILK. SILK IS AN AMAZINGLY STRONG MATERIAL —STRONGER THAN STEEL. SPIDERS USE IT FOR ...

* Building webs and traps
* Sensing vibrations
* Wrapping up prey
* Safety lines (like a safety harness)
* Parachutes
* Egg sacs
* Mating (the male gives the female a gift of some food wrapped up in silk)

FIVE TYPES OF
INSECT THAT MAKE SILK:

1. Weaver ants
2. Caddisfly larvae
3. Bumblebee larvae
4. Silkworm larvae
   (these are moths)
5. Many other
   moth larvae

Lots of bugs have a
venomous sting or bite.
But bombardier beetles
fight off attackers
by squirting

BOILING
HOT ACID

at them.

Some kinds of

TARANTULA

have bristly itchy hairs on their body, which they flick at predators as a defense weapon. The hairs are so itchy that the predator gives up on trying to catch the spider. Sometimes the itchy hairs even kill the predator.

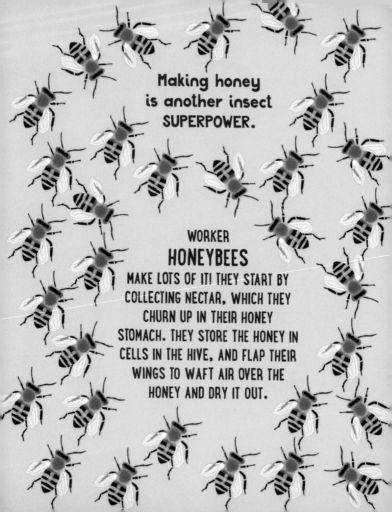

**Making honey
is another insect
SUPERPOWER.**

WORKER

HONEYBEES

MAKE LOTS OF IT! THEY START BY
COLLECTING NECTAR, WHICH THEY
CHURN UP IN THEIR HONEY
STOMACH. THEY STORE THE HONEY IN
CELLS IN THE HIVE, AND FLAP THEIR
WINGS TO WAFT AIR OVER THE
HONEY AND DRY IT OUT.

People have kept bees for **thousands of years** so they can enjoy honey. Honey 3,500 years old was found in ancient Egyptian pharaoh Tutankhamun's tomb.

Ancient Romans used honey to TREAT WOUNDS.

Bumblebees and some
wasps also make small
amounts of honey.

HONEYPOT ANTS

make honey too. They start with honeydew,
a sugary liquid that oozes out of greenfly.
Lots of ants eat honeydew, but some
honeypot ants eat so much that their
bodies swell up like a round
berry. Then, when there are not
many greenfly around, worker
ants stroke the swollen
ants until they vomit
honey for the
workers to eat!

worker ant

117

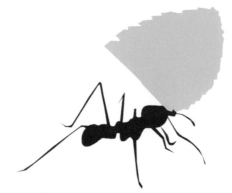

IN TROPICAL RAINFORESTS,

LEAFCUTTER ANTS

CARRY LEAVES TO THE NEST,
THEN THE ANTS CHEW THEM
UP A BIT AND LET FUNGUS
GROW ON THEM. THEY FEED THE
FUNGUS TO THEIR LARVAE.

LEAFCUTTER ANTS HAVE
JAWS LIKE CHAINSAWS
AND CAN CARRY THINGS
THAT ARE 50 TIMES
HEAVIER THAN THEY ARE.

119

SOME INSECTS HAVE CLEVER WAYS TO KEEP WARM OR COOL. THEY USE IMPRESSIVE ENGINEERING TECHNOLOGY!

Butterflies warm up by using their wings like SOLAR PANELS. They bask in the sunshine with their wings open, heating their blood.

WOOD ANTS
KNOW HOW TO BUILD
A CENTRAL HEATING SYSTEM. THEY KEEP THEIR NEST WARM BY BUILDING IT AROUND A ROTTING TREE STUMP. AS THE WOOD ROTS, HEAT IS GIVEN OFF AND THIS KEEPS THE NEST WARM.

121

WASPS keep their nests cool by sitting at the
entrance and using their wings to WAFT COOL AIR
INSIDE, and by collecting water and spitting
it out on the nest walls to cool it down.

TERMITES DESIGN CLEVER, COMPLICATED AIR-CONDITIONING SYSTEMS. THEY BUILD LOTS OF TUNNELS, CHIMNEYS, AND WINDOWS SO THAT AIR CAN FLOW AROUND THE TERMITE MOUND. OUTSIDE IT GETS HOT IN THE DAYTIME AND COOL AT NIGHT, BUT IN THE MOUND THE TEMPERATURE STAYS ABOUT THE SAME.

SPIDERS

can climb up walls and
CLING UPSIDE-DOWN
onto ceilings. They have
special **BROOM-LIKE HAIRS**
on their feet, which work like
suckers on smooth surfaces.

Pond skaters
and raft spiders
can walk on water.
They both have
water-repellent feet
that allow them to
skate on top of
the water rather
than sinking.

BEES, ANTS, HOVERFLIES, BUTTERFLIES, AND MOTHS are pollination superstars. Flowering plants make pollen, and they need the pollen to be moved from one flower to another so they can make seeds for new plants to grow. Most plants rely on animals—especially insects—for pollination.

One kind of bee found in the southwestern US can pollinate about 50,000 BLUEBERRY FLOWERS in her few weeks of life.

FEMALE BITING MIDGES suck people's blood but the males sip nectar and pollinate plants including cacao, the plant that gives us chocolate!

BUGS MAKE UP

part of the world's superhero
army of decomposers.

These are living things that break down
dead animals, dead leaves and other
bits of plants, and poop. They recycle
all this material into useful
chemicals, which go back into the
soil and in turn help plants to grow.

SIX DECOMPOSER BUGS:

1. Burying beetles
2. Dung beetles
3. Fly larvae (maggots)
4. Millipedes
5. Wood-eating beetle larvae
6. Woodlice

Record Breaking Bugs

Which is the BIGGEST INSECT?

Experts can't agree. Here are some contenders:

THE TITAN BEETLE OF THE AMAZON RAINFOREST IS 6.3 IN. LONG.

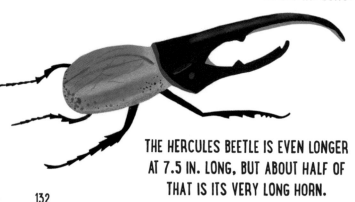

THE HERCULES BEETLE IS EVEN LONGER AT 7.5 IN. LONG, BUT ABOUT HALF OF THAT IS ITS VERY LONG HORN.

IN AFRICA, THE GOLIATH BEETLE LARVA IS EVEN HEAVIER. IT WEIGHS 2.8–3.5 OZ., BUT THE ADULT IS ONLY HALF AS BIG, AT 4.7 IN. LONG.

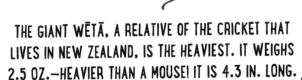

THE GIANT WĒTĀ, A RELATIVE OF THE CRICKET THAT LIVES IN NEW ZEALAND, IS THE HEAVIEST. IT WEIGHS 2.5 OZ.–HEAVIER THAN A MOUSE! IT IS 4.3 IN. LONG.

The
BIGGEST
butterfly is a female
QUEEN
ALEXANDRA'S
BIRDWING

It has a wingspan
of nearly 11 in.—wider
than this open book.

Queen Alexandra's
birdwing

The biggest spider is
the GOLIATH BIRDEATER,
a tarantula found in the
Amazon rainforest. It has
a leg span of 11 in. and
weighs up to 6 oz.

The GIANT CENTIPEDE, a ferocious predator found in the Amazon rainforest, is nearly 12 in. long. It eats insects, tarantulas, birds, lizards, rodents, and even snakes.

THE FASTEST ...

ANT–SAHARAN SILVER ANT
1,913 mph - 20 times faster
than the fastest human sprinter

**BUTTERFLY–
SKIPPERS**
31 mph

BEETLE–TIGER BEETLE
5 mph - 125 times its own
body length per second

FLY–HORSEFLY
90 mph

**DRAGONFLY–SOUTHERN GIANT
DARNER** 18 mph

MOTH–HAWK MOTH
12 mph

Jumping spiders can jump
100 times their body length.
Fleas can leap even more
than 100 times theirs.

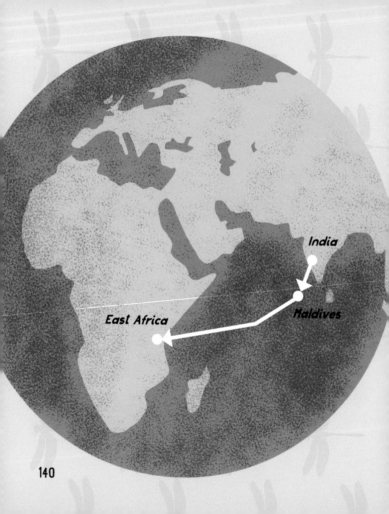

India

Maldives

East Africa

The globe skimmer dragonfly makes the longest journey of any insect. Every year these record breakers migrate from **INDIA** to **EAST AFRICA**, stopping off at the Maldives on the way. The round trip is an amazing 11,000 mi. Each individual dragonfly flies around **3,700 KM** of the journey.

The **SCHMIDT'S STING PAIN INDEX** is a way of measuring how painful a bite or sting is. **THE WARRIOR WASP, BULLET ANT, AND TARANTULA HAWK WASP** all score top marks, making them officially the world's most painful insects.

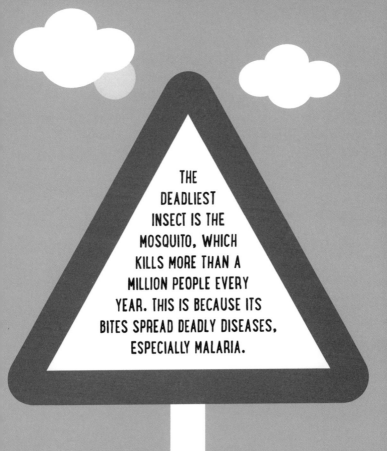

THE DEADLIEST INSECT IS THE MOSQUITO, WHICH KILLS MORE THAN A MILLION PEOPLE EVERY YEAR. THIS IS BECAUSE ITS BITES SPREAD DEADLY DISEASES, ESPECIALLY MALARIA.

The biggest insect ever was *MEGANEURA*, a PREHISTORIC DRAGONFLY with a wingspan of 28 in.